Common Bond

Real Stories of Struggles and Successes Inspired by the Album

Presented to:

From:

Date:

Common Bond

First printing: September 2007

ISBN 13: 978-0-89221-679-6
ISBN 10: 0-89221-679-4
Library of Congress Control Number: 2007925413

Cover design by Jayme Brandt, Twice Born, Eureka Springs, AR

All images from istockphoto.com and photos.com except for personal submissions.

Printed in Italy

Please visit our website for other great titles: www.newleafpress.net

For information regarding author interviews please contact the publicity department at (870) 438-5228

New Leaf Press

Table of Contents

Introduction: *Jill Laffoon*......................................9

Chapter 1: *One Day*......................................12

Chapter 2: *God is a Dreamer*......................................22

Chapter 3: *Let It Rain*......................................32

Chapter 4: *I Believe*......................................44

Chapter 5: *Common Bond*......................................52

Chapter 6: *This Is The Beginning*......................................62

Chapter 7: *Forgiven*......................................76

Chapter 8: *Worthy After All*......................................86

Chapter 9: *I Am Holding You*......................................98

Chapter 10: *I Sing*......................................112

Ministry Photos......................................122

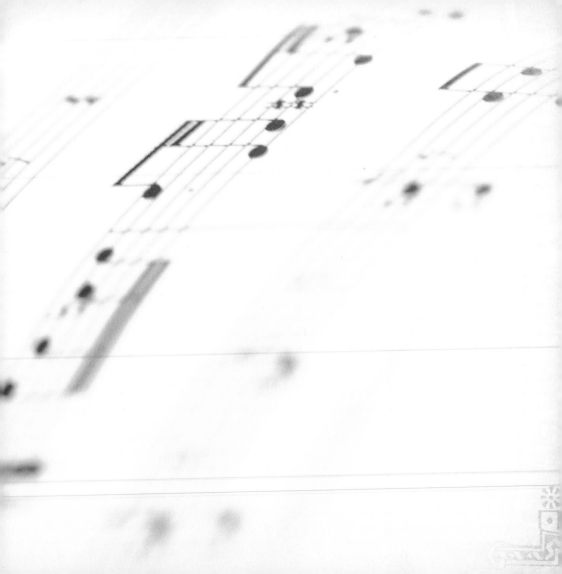

INTRODUCTION *by Jill Laffoon*

The concept for this book came during a seminar for Sunday school teachers and pastors. Todd Braschler and I had spent an enjoyable morning at our "booth" meeting staff members from churches across the state. Our initial purpose in attending the event was to meet key church leaders and introduce them to the music and message of Todd Braschler Ministries. Additionally, Todd was providing a conference on transitioning churches in worship. We were having a terrific time chatting with people and meeting new friends. . . .

Around noon, Todd taught a "breakout session" to music ministers designed to help them grow their music ministry; change is difficult in any arena, but in many churches the songs and style of worship are battlegrounds for change. It is a difficult balance, to add new dimension to morning worship, and retain the spirit of the original elements. Todd's message on that day was titled something like "Transitions in Worship!" The premise was that as a music ministry, you can grow and change without completely sacrificing the old standards that are well loved and received . . . sometimes you just have to come up with a new way to include them.

Now, I was privileged to have been a member of Todd's Sunday school class years ago and have heard him speak many times, so there is really no reason for me to be surprised at the depth and enthusiasm he brings to a message. But every time I hear him, I am amazed at the clarity he can give to God's Word and I always leave feeling completely rejuvenated. On this day, the message was not one which I expected to ever use . . . if there were only three people left in a church, I can guarantee you that two of them would make better music ministers than would I. So I frankly sat in on the session as more of a break from the "booth" than anything else. I should have known better — within five minutes I was taking notes, and at the end of the session I was so ready to take on any life change that might come my way that I might have spent the afternoon trying to think one up . . . but for one thing: I asked Todd how I got something out of a message that was designed for music ministers in a specific quandary. His answer, instead of a predictable, "Well, that is what God wanted you to hear" was more along the lines of "You know how when you eat a lollipop and when you are finished you look in the mirror and you can still see the color on your tongue? Well, I want my communications to be like that. That is what I pray . . . no matter the topic, that everyone would walk away with a little something that stays with them for a while." Basically, he said, "That is what God wanted you to hear," but in typical Todd B. fashion, his original delivery really made an impression — so to speak.

Later that afternoon we began chatting about the new recording project Todd had completed, *Common Bond*. Todd and his wife, Claudia, and my husband,

Todd, and I had spent hours listening to demo songs before we selected the tunes that are now on the CD.

I was still thinking about the lollipop stain on my tongue when I said, "You know, what I really love is that people relate to the songs on *Common Bond* so well . . . sometimes I can see the emotion in people as they hear the words to different songs. These people really took something away after hearing you sing."

Todd nodded and said, "I love to tell the story about how 'Worthy After All' was written. People tell me all the time that they lived that life, that they felt unworthy . . . and they pause and weep to think that 1) they are worthy and 2) that someone else has been in a similar situation."

What followed was one of those "duh" moments: we both realized that the very reason we chose these songs was because of their relevance to real situations. And so the idea for the devotional was born; for each of the songs we would find someone willing to share a personal testimony that illustrated the principle of the lyrics.

God is a humorist. We began the CD project with a grand mission: "To honor God's unlimited vision." We really had no idea how unlimited his vision was — where we thought we would educate, we've been educated; where we thought we would inspire, we've been inspired.

You have heard the CD, but the real voices are contained within these pages. We have been humbled and blessed by the submissions for this book and our lasting prayer is that when you are finished with the reading, you will still see the color it left on you.

One Day

— Jeff Silvey and Reggie Hamm

Stirring in our soul is a feeling so strong,
A light of faith and hope that sets us free.
Living everyday in a place we don't belong,
Longing for a place we've never seen
Beyond our wildest dreams.

Chorus:
One day we'll walk, in fields of heaven's glory
With the one who wrote the story.
One day we'll stand, amazed at all his graces
And we'll sing a million praises, one day.

Days turn into weeks, months turn into years.
Isn't it funny how time flies?
All we do is dream of somewhere far from here.
We've got heaven on our hearts and minds
When we open up our eyes.

The home of the angels
And the wishes of all our hearts
Will someday come together.
The tears will be dry as soon as eternity starts.

One Day

Wasn't it a ketchup commercial on TV in the 70s that illustrated so well the emotion of anticipation? I can still hear that lady singing, "Anticipation, anticipa-a-a-tion, it's making me wait. It's keeping me waiting." The poor soul in the commercial is seated in the kitchen with a ketchup bottle tipped up, trying to douse a hamburger with tomato flavor. Why don't they make commercials like that anymore?

I remember after moving to Florida from Indiana my parents took me and my two brothers and sister to Busch Gardens for the first time. My father was pastor of a church in Tampa, Florida in 1971, around the time when an amusement park was added to the brewery on Busch Boulevard in Tampa. After paying to enter the park, we could hardly wait to see it! News and TV had pronounced its coming and kids at school could hardly stop talking about the newest ride added to the park — the Python. This ride consisted of three full corkscrew twists at an average speed of 60 miles per hour. There was nothing like it in our area, and we had never seen anything like this ride before.

Just like an old-fashioned roller coaster, the Python began innocently with the tick-tick-tick of the tracks as it hoisted us higher and higher before the exhilarating first launch. My heart began to pound so loudly I could hardly hear the screaming of my sister seated next to me. We raised our hands high in the air (half-heartedly, of course) and off we went. The snake-like series of cars zoomed down toward the earth, into the corkscrews, up and around, faster and faster. I actually heard myself scream higher than my sister, I'm sorry to admit. Talk about a thrill! I had never felt anything like it in my life. The kids at school were right. A couple of years ago I re-visited the same park with my family and children. To my surprise, the Python was still there — but it looked like a kiddie ride compared to the rides now making Busch Gardens a huge tourist attraction.

I look back on that experience and remember the anticipation of this ride even while moving to Florida with my family from Anderson, Indiana. I was bound and determined to experience every exciting moment of the Python. The great enthusiasm and expectation for Busch Gardens eased the pain of leaving friends in Ms. Russell's third grade class at Franklin Elementary.

"One Day" was chosen as a final statement of God's reward for the many messages presented in this project. The words encourage us to look with great anticipation to the day we meet the author of our life face to face.

Each day has so much greater significance when lived in expectation of that great meeting. May our lives exude the excitement and anticipation of seeing our Savior, the author of our story.

One Day

Julie Skillman *is one of
those rare individuals that those of us
less gifted often visit with, thinking we'll
lift their spirits, even encourage them
a bit. Then upon leaving or hanging
up the phone or otherwise ending
the conversation, we humbly realize that the opposite has occurred — she has lifted our spirits
— she spent the entire time somehow quietly encouraging the encourager. Mrs. Skillman lives in
Casper, Wyoming, where she spends as much time as possible with her family — especially her
four grandchildren. She and her husband, Al, attend Highland Park Community Church. Their
connection with Todd came between 1994 and 1998 while Todd served as the music pastor at
Highland Park Community Church in Casper, Wyoming. Al sang in the Sanctuary Choir and Julie
was very involved in women's ministry.*

The phone rang on a Sunday night and a doctor informed me that I had
ovarian cancer — he asked me if I knew anything about it and I said I didn't think
it was the one that you would choose to have. He said, "You're right." Ovarian
cancer is the most deadly of gynecological cancers. I wasn't afraid to die. I just

didn't want to die now; we had just found out that our daughter was expecting our first grandchild — would I live to see her? *Would she ever know me?*

I knew in whom I could trust — I'd been there before. My mother passed away when I was a teenager. My father, who was my dearest friend and my spiritual and life mentor, died when I was in my 30s — followed by my brother, who left a wife and three young children. Yes, my faith had been tested and I knew it worked; I just didn't know what a workout my faith would be receiving.

Four days of tests, CT scans, x-rays, and ultrasound were non-conclusive. Surgery determined advanced ovarian cancer. I went to God for assurance, stability, and shelter and to find comfort in all the things they were doing to me. Daytime seemed so dark, and nights even darker . . . it is in the dark that Satan does his best work. God wrapped His arms around me in the tough times.

Former pastor and president of the Moody Bible Institute Joseph Stowell says, "God is the sovereign sentinel at the door of our lives." I love that — it means that He okays everything that goes in and out — and if it is okay with Him, then it is okay with me.

Chemotherapy followed the diagnosis. Four months later, I had an angioplasty for a blocked artery. Eight months later, colon cancer was discovered. The colon cancer was removed surgically, but the night before I was dismissed from the hospital two of my doctors came to my room to tell me that the ovarian cancer had returned.

Once ovarian cancer returns, the general diagnosis is that there will be no cure. Medical personnel focus on "salvage therapy."

I discovered that God is more interested in our character than our comfort. I underwent a second round of chemotherapy. I lost my hair, my eyelashes, my eyebrows, and (in my mind) my identity. It isn't so much vanity — it is just a desire to be normal. During treatment five I had a sharp pain. My bowel had ruptured. Because of the chemo, I had no resistance — which I desperately needed after bowel surgery. I lost weight; at 5'10", I was down to about 110 pounds and hairless. I read Psalms 42 and 43, "Why be discouraged and sad? Hope in God! I shall yet praise him again. Yes I shall praise Him for His help . . . *expect God to act!* For I know that I shall again have plenty of reason to praise Him for all that He will do. He is my help! He is my God! Trust in God! I shall again praise him for His wondrous help: He will make me to smile again, for He is my God!" (paraphrase).

Six months later, several people, including a doctor, told me they hadn't expected me to live . . . I did, of course, and I did smile again. Many more scares were to follow: I heard these horrible words, "This is no longer curable." I lost my hair again. And again.

The two to (maybe) four years I was given to live following my first diagnosis has extended to nearly nine. Doctors are amazed. I tell them that I probably have 1,000 people praying for me. One doctor said, "Tell them not to quit." I've had 16 surgeries, 6 angioplasties, and over 100 chemo treatments with some pretty monumental side effects. I tell you this not so you can see where I have been, but so you can see how faithful and trustworthy God has been.

At least once a week I lie on my couch and look around at everything and say, "Exactly what am I taking with me to heaven?" Too frequently we get so involved in our "stuff" here, that heaven slips our mind. **One Day** we'll be there.

I became a Christian as a preschooler in a home where heaven was frequently discussed. Heaven seems to be talked about much less nowadays — except in the chemo lab. When it comes to cancer patients, even non-Christians listen to any talk of God or heaven or how you know you are getting there. The word "cancer" gets your attention. Death and its processes scare you and me. The fact of heaven as a real place becomes even more alive to us. And it's not that we don't want to go there, it is just that none of us want to leave here. When we finally do arrive, we'll wonder what kept us here, why we worked so hard to stay on earth.

Cancer and the ensuing heart problems have made heaven even more real to me . . . and I get excited about it. However, I would still like to go up with the rest of you.

"Heaven is the only thing solid, the only thing permanent, the only thing you can be certain about. Never let earth eclipse the reality of heaven, lean towards heaven, live on earth from that perspective" (Howard Stowell).

One Day (maybe today) we'll walk, we'll stand, we'll sing in our real home: the one where we belong. Can we trust this God of ours? More than ever, He is so TRUSTWORTHY! **ONE DAY,** be there!

God is a Dreamer

— Jeff Silvey, Robert Ellis, Orrall & Kim Williams

Before the day that we were born
God had a perfect plan.
Through His wisdom, by His grace,
Our future's in His hands.
Though right now it seems to us
Such a mystery,
If we keep our eyes on Him,
One day we will see

Chorus:
God is a dreamer
And we are the dream.
He's a believer
That we all can be redeemed.
With heavenly visions
Of what all we can be,
God is a dreamer,
And we are the dream.
In this life we're pressing on
Toward a higher call.
One day He'll show us everything,
And we'll understand it all.
Until then there's comfort in
His mercy and his love,
And when we see forever,
We'll know we're waking up.

God is a Dreamer

If there's one thing kids constantly find themselves in trouble for, it's asking too many questions. "When will we be there?" "Why are frogs green?" "Will I be able to see you after you die and become an angel?" Many of these questions I should not attempt to answer for fear that my ignorance will be discovered. And yet, this is probably just how many of us will spend eternity in heaven someday — asking questions. "Why did you allow that to happen?" "What were you thinking when you built the Grand Canyon?" "Why did I have to wait till heaven to have the ability to fly?" You know: important questions.

One of the greatest challenges in living a life in Christ is trying to figure Him out; to understand how God thinks, how He always sees something deeper, wider, and more positive in situations and people than I do. This a constant challenge — to see the world, others, my life, and circumstances through the eyes of God.

"God is a Dreamer" was chosen for this project because of the profound call to view the world with the passion and vision of God.

This song is a call to each of us to trust God with His plan for us.

In Jeremiah 29:11, we read: "For I know the thoughts that I think toward you, saith the LORD, thoughts of peace, and not of evil, to give you an expected end" (KJV).

God dreams about me. Can we wrap our minds around this overwhelming statement? God has such passion for you and me that even the marvelous elements of His creation pale in comparison to His passion and dream for His children. To think this way requires a renewed mind, a very different vision for the purpose of my life and those around me than what may come naturally to me.

Romans 12:2 encourages this type of thinking:

Do not conform any longer to the pattern of this world, but be transformed by the renewing of your **mind***. Then you will be able to test and approve what God's will is — his good, pleasing and perfect will* (NIV).

"Dear God, I pray for the kind of vision that brings wisdom to others. I pray for unusual insight into situations and circumstances we see around us every day. May we desire greater ways to envision Your purposes for the people and activities around us; to be the voice of hope where the world would prescribe doom and disaster. Draw us closer to You that we may know the dream You have for us. Amen."

"But God hath chosen the foolish things of the world to **confound** the wise; and God hath chosen the weak things of the world to **confound** the things which are mighty"

(1 Cor. 1:27; KJV).

God is a Dreamer

Todd Braschler *is an avid hunter, fisherman, and Kentucky Wildcat fan who lives in Wichita, Kansas, with his wife of 19 years, Claudia. Todd and Claudia are blessed and outnumbered by three sons: Nick, Tyler, and Jacob. They have two freezers, two hunting dogs, a miniature dachshund named Rusty, and an amazing variety of sports equipment. They shop at Sam's a lot and are prone to lots of eye rolling and odd bursts of laughter.*

Can you name someone in your past who helped re-define how you saw yourself? In God's great wisdom and love for me, He placed many individuals in my life path to ensure a greater vision for my future.

Being raised as a preacher's kid, God began my life under the influence of two perfect parents. Not really, but they sure seemed that way growing up, and even more so after I had my own children. These were two people who would not allow mediocre thinking or status quo attitudes. This was so important in childhood for a skinny, shy, unhealthy young kid. I recall a sermon my father preached during my high school years where he recalled putting me to bed as an infant not knowing if my life would continue the following morning due to a life-threatening illness. I realized then that my parents were the first to sense that God had something He was saving me for. I was re-defined with a new vision and sense of call that God wanted to use my life in a special way after that sermon.

Raised in a home of strong personalities and as the oldest of four children, all equally strong, a blurred picture of someone less gifted and vivacious began to emerge during my early high school years. Satan began to lie to me about my potential and ability. During my sophomore year in high school I tried out for the football team; I was a strapping physical specimen of 6'1" and 132 pounds — with pads on! I actually think they put me on the offensive line just to make me quit. I was immediately aware that I had stepped into a world where I did not belong: I was compelled to prove them wrong.

Coach Green, our head coach for the football team at John F. Hodge High School in St. James, Missouri, was a driving personality. I couldn't tell if he actually believed in me, or just enjoyed placing me in lethal situations on the playing field.

One day, during a drill we called the "hamburger drill," my life took a drastic turn — really. In this particular practice drill often used, two players were placed head to head on their backs across from one another. Kevin K. was the guy with the ball. Our objective was to jump off the ground on the whistle, shed the blocker, John, and hit the ball carrier, Kevin, before he could reach a line of padded dummies. With the grace of an inebriated elephant, I somehow spun out of the grasp of my opponent John, and caught the running back behind the line for a clean and lightening fast tackle (this scene grows in my mind even as I write). What a thrill! Right in front of everyone, I had proven I was more than skin and

bones — I had aggression and power and heart. Before I could stand to my feet, the entire team was applauding. Since I had never experienced anything positive in the game of football, I joined in the applause not exactly knowing what we were applauding. To my amazement, Coach Green was actually leading the cheer. In front of everyone he shouted, "Braschler, you are the most improved player on this team!" It should go without saying, from that day forward I played the game of football with the vision and passion of a 245-pound linebacker. While I never did start or make a huge impact for our team, Coach Green spoke words into me that day that forever changed the way I defined my potential. If I could have success for even just a moment, in something at which I was seemingly so inept, I could overcome anything and accomplish anything!

While this story even now makes my heart pump on a double-time beat, it pales in comparison to my Heavenly Father and His belief in me. God has taken me from questioning my personal abilities to opportunities to lead others to Him, to serving as a pastor, worship leader, teacher, singer, consultant, father, and husband. Most of these opportunities, if not all, were far beyond what I ever saw, but God's vision was obviously far different than my own.

The thought I ponder today is the vision of God, the Father, in heaven, dreaming and thinking about me. I'm challenged every day to see myself with the same vision that my parents did. I'm challenged to remember Coach Green's powerful words. I'm challenged to remember that God is so passionate about His children. I'm challenged to remember that heaven is nothing to God without the company of His children. I'm comforted and encouraged to know that in the midst of perfection in heaven, *God dreams about my imperfect life and His plan for me.*

Let it Rain

— Jeff Silvey and Wendy Wills

In this field of faith my arms are open wide,
On my knees, staring at the sky,
Waiting, longing, praying You will hear my cry.
Open up Your hand and I'll be satisfied.

Chorus:
Let it rain, pour Your Holy Spirit down on me.
Let it rain, falling from the Father,
The taste of living water pure and sweet.
Let it rain.

Hope is gathering like the clouds inside of me;
Winds of expectations stir my soul.
You can flood me with Your mercy
Till I'm drowning deep;
It would only leave me wanting more and more.

Open up your hand, Lord.
Open up your hand, Lord.

Let it Rain

From 1994–1998, I had the privilege of serving as the worship pastor at the Highland Park Community Church in Casper, Wyoming. JoAnn T. led the drama ministry there with excellence and passion and still does to this day. On one particular Sunday during the Thanksgiving season, JoAnn organized a drama sketch about the Thanksgiving meal. While I can't remember the title, I'll never forget the message:

A family of three, a mom and dad and their daughter, were seated at the dinner table preparing to serve the Thanksgiving meal. There seemed to be a tremendous amount of tension in this home in every relationship present. Bickering and complaining about the food and the cold temperatures during Thanksgiving created an atmosphere that wasn't very thankful. When everyone was finally seated around the table, the father bowed his head and invited his family to pray with him. In the midst of thanking God for the food and whatever else he could thank God for, the father asked God to be with his family during this special holiday dinner.

As the food was passed and the sound of china clanking against porcelain filled the room, a man dressed like Jesus suddenly appeared from back stage. He seemed invisible to the family, but certainly grabbed the attention of the audience. The character of Jesus seemed to be listening to the family as they continued to badger one another. They began complaining about the food and criticizing their friends who were not present. Jesus then moved toward each of the family members, touching them on the shoulder as they spoke. At the moment of his touch, the person speaking quickly changed the direction of the conversation to resemble more the attitude of Christ. Compassion replaced criticism. Tenderness replaced anger and frustration. The audience witnessed a complete change in the language, posture, and attitude of each participant through a simple touch.

This drama so well describes those of us who often take for granted the fact that we can ask for the presence of God in our families and our lives. We can

often forget that God hears our prayers and actually shows up on occasion to bless our gatherings, our meals, and our circumstances.

"Let It Rain" is one of the most anointed songs God has ever allowed me to sing. This song so adequately expresses, through the metaphor of rain, the infilling and penetrating power of the Holy Spirit, and the power of His presence.

The second verse gives us an idea of the type of atmosphere the Holy Spirit loves to reside in — a sense of expectancy. It also describes the unquenchable appetite created once we've been in the presence of the Holy Spirit — we can't get enough. I love pizza, but I am often filled up quickly. I love vacation, but I'm ready to come home in a week or less. But when it comes to the Holy Spirit, His power and His wisdom, I can never have my appetite quenched — I can never get enough. This song was chosen to encourage the Church to dream about the Church God dreams about with confidence and vision. See the future and potential of the Church and of your life through the eyes of God and with the power of the Holy Spirit.

"Now it is God who has made us for this very purpose and has given us the Spirit as a deposit, guaranteeing what is to come" (2 Cor. 5:5; NIV).

Let It Rain

Darlene McCulley *is
a recent single parent of four children.
She and her two youngest daughters live
in Maize, Kansas. Her daughter Ellen
introduced Darlene to Todd through
her friendship with Todd's oldest son,
Nick. Darlene is pictured here with her
husband, Mike, and their four children
(l-r) Laura, Michael, Ellen, and Carol. She works as a family practice nurse in Wichita and attends the
Westlink Christian Church with her family. The McCulley family attends the same church as the Braschler
family.*

Darlene McCulley's voice is quiet and steady as she speaks about the loss of her
husband of 24 years; she clasps her hands in her lap, sometimes visibly squeezing them
as she describes difficulties and pain. She is so petite, but the strength behind her words
— behind her body language — is startling. When she smiles, it is slightly sad and fierce
and passionate at the same time.

She takes a deep breath and tells her story: "It crushes you," she says of receiving news that her husband, Mike, had 3 to 18 months to live. After 5 months of trying to diagnose the cause of an apparent infection in his gastrointestinal tract, the news in May of 2001 that Mike, 51, had pancreatic cancer was devastating. As medical professionals (Mike, Director of Employee Health and Human Resources at a local hospital and Darlene, a registered nurse), the McCulleys knew the diagnosis guaranteed that their life as a family would be irreversibly changed. "Pancreatic cancer is rare," Darlene explains, "and the statistics are grim." Still, Mike seemed a contender to beat the odds of the disease. He did well with treatments and life seemed somewhat normal. He was, as he had always been, "a rock" for his family.

"I have to describe him as a man of such faith [in God], he never wavered," Darlene explains. "Right at the beginning, Mike told me and told the kids, '#1 — our hope is in the Lord; #2 — this is no surprise to Him, it is all a part of His perfect plan; #3—the number of my days on earth has not changed from the beginning of time. God has always known how long I would be here.' "

In the spring of 2002, blood levels showed the cancer at low levels. "God is working," Darlene recalls Mike telling the doctor as they waited out the summer (and a bout with pneumonia), hoping that their insurance would approve their request for a visit to the University of Texas M.D. Anderson Cancer Center in Houston, Texas. When they finally made the trip, their doctor told them he thought he could remove the tumor, taking about 1/3 of Mike's stomach and 1/3 of his small intestine.

Surgery was on September 24, 2002. Darlene and daughters Carol and Ellen were in Houston with Mike. Michael, away at college, and Laura, home in Maize, tried to continue life as usual. "Our church family was — is — incredible," says Darlene of the members of Westlink Christian Church in Wichita who prayed and helped out the family during Mike's illness. "I was able to stay in Houston for three weeks."

Mike returned to Kansas in late October. He was very ill. Darlene sighs, "He couldn't keep food down, and he was in pain." She raises her hand, palm up, as she explains the surgery, "We wanted to get the cancer out." Mike's doctors did not feel that they'd removed enough of the cancer to expect results from chemotherapy. They struggled

through the winter with Mike still losing weight and without energy. Blood tests were not encouraging.

In January 2003, a CAT scan revealed that the cancer had spread to the liver. The oncologist — whom Mike had named "Mr. Happy Face" for his lack of smiles — gave Mike three to six months. "You keep hoping," Darlene says earnestly. "We kept hoping that God would turn it around and heal him." In March of 2003, after Mike reluctantly retired from his job at Via Christi Hospital, the family took a cruise together.

"It was great," Darlene smiles, "all of the kids got to go. Mike rested a lot. . . ."

The family was together again for Easter and then the older children returned to college, as Darlene continued caring for Mike and their two younger daughters. "Mike got very quiet those last few months," Darlene says, taking a deep breath. "I missed our conversations."

In late April, Darlene knew things were worsening. "On a Monday night, he was so ill. He fell out of bed and I couldn't get him back in. On Tuesday, Hospice came."

On Friday morning, May 2, 2003, Darlene McCulley sat beside her husband. "He'd been pretty peaceful," she recalls, "I just felt like I needed to tell him we were okay. I said, 'Honey, you go on and be with Jesus. We'll be fine. The kids and I will be fine.' Five minutes later he slipped away."

"It is so hard," Darlene says, tears filling her eyes, "to not be able to fix it, or to make a difference. "I made a decision that I would not be bitter; Mike said it early on, 'God had chosen this path for us.' And how could I be bitter? I looked back at all of the blessings that God had given us in 24 years. All of the good times. How could I discount all that He had done for us?"

" 'Let It Rain' is our story.

"Affliction comes. It comes to all of us. My husband was very good with people; very relational. He loved people. He had such a ministry in life — and I saw God pour out blessings like rain on us in those two years (of Mike's illness). It was as if God had a barrel pouring out blessings, provisions, and support. 'Let It Rain' is about satisfaction and hope.

"Half of me is gone, sort of. There is a lot of empty space in me. I'm looking to God to satisfy me in a new way and fill that space — and He is doing it, day by day. Hope carried us through. You can't live apart from hope. I hoped that God would heal Mike. Now my hope is for whatever is good for my family. Whatever new hope He has for us, we'll take.

"Early on, a prayer that Mike and I had through this illness is that God would get the glory — this book is a way for this to happen. You can trust God through all things. He is over all, in all, through all. And He can be trusted even if the outcome is not what we want."

I Believe

— Morgan Cryar

I have this faith, it seems so tiny;
And all my need just seems so great.
And I have this love, still I'm so unloving;
You've shown me patience, still it's so hard to wait.

Chorus
But I believe, help my unbelief.
I am yours, so Lord, take all of me.
I am healed, though my heart is all that sees it.

I believe.
I believe, help my unbelief.

You've been so true, while I've been unfaithful;
You gave me your word, still I'm so unsure.
You gave me your spirit, but there's always a battle;
You burn in my heart Lord, so don't stop till it's pure.

Lord, show me how you see,
Let this prison heart go free.
Let me know that you're not
Through with me, yeah.

I Believe

I met a wonderful Christian artist by the name of Morgan Cryar during a vocal competition held in Wichita, Kansas, in 2001. This was a powerful introduction for me, having heard Morgan's music for many years. During this particular month, my wife, Claudia, and I, with our friends, Todd and Jill Laffoon, were all praying desperately for a sign from God that it was time for me to pursue this area of my calling. It seemed pretty strange that God would wait until I was in my late 30s and a father of three sons to call me into this type of ministry. I had tried to persuade God toward this direction some 17 years before to no avail; God just kept coming back with the same answer, "I have plenty of singers out there. I need more artists who actually have something to sing about." God used these past 17 years to solidify a passion and message in me. Morgan's vocal competition came along the first of June, and after winning the grand prize (a recording project just three weeks after this competition in his studio in Nashville), we sensed we had

46

the first part of our confirmation that the time was right. Just three weeks after this competition, with only eight concerts booked, I resigned as the Assimilation Pastor at Central Community Church in Wichita.

During the recording sessions in Morgan's studio, he requested that I listen to a song he had written some time back called "I Believe." Morgan's gifts for ministry were powerfully evident in this song. When he offered me the privilege to be the first artist to record it, I couldn't pass it up! It was at that moment that the words to this song laid a faith-foundation for the year to come for our ministry.

The Book of Mark, chapter nine, verses 14–27, offers the foundation and inspiration for this song.

When they came to the other disciples, they saw a large crowd around them and the teachers of the law arguing with them. As soon as all the people saw Jesus, they were overwhelmed with wonder and ran to greet him.

"What are you arguing with them about?" he asked.

A man in the crowd answered, "Teacher, I brought you my son, who is possessed by a spirit that has robbed him of speech. Whenever it seizes him, it throws him to the ground. He foams at the mouth, gnashes his teeth and becomes rigid. I asked your disciples to drive out the spirit but they could not."

"O unbelieving generations," Jesus replied, "how long shall I stay with you? How long shall I put up with you? Bring the boy to me."

So they brought him. When the Spirit saw Jesus, it immediately threw the boy into a convulsion. He fell to the ground and rolled around, foaming at the mouth.

Jesus asked the boy's father, "How long has he been like this?"

"From childhood," he answered. "It has often thrown him into fire or water to kill him. But if you can do anything, take pity on us and help us."

"If you can?" said Jesus. "Everything is possible for him who believes."

Immediately the boy's father exclaimed, "I do believe; help me overcome my unbelief!"

When Jesus saw that a crowd was running to the scene, he rebuked the evil spirit. "You deaf and mute spirit," he said, "I command you, come out of him and never enter him again."

The spirit shrieked, convulsed him violently and came out. The boy looked so much like a corpse that many said, "He's dead." But Jesus took him by the hand and lifted him to his feet and he stood up (NIV).

Thank you to Morgan for these modern day words to apply an eternal story in Scripture. Show me a person who hasn't been in situations where they've questioned their faith, and I'll show you a person who desperately needs to take a risk, and soon.

I Believe

Gracia Burnham

and her children live in Rosehill, Kansas, where Gracia calls home
base for her book writing, missionary, and speaking ministry.
Following a tragic event in the life of her family, Gracia became a
nationally recognized example of courage and faith. Her connection
with Todd Braschler came through an inquiry to include her
dramatic story in this collection of life stories. She has become a dear friend to us, and such a blessing to
thousands of others. We are honored to offer her testimony in this collection.

My name is **Gracia Burnham**. My husband, Martin, and I were missionaries in the Philippines for 16 years. On May 27, 2001, we were abducted by Muslim terrorists and spent the next year and several weeks living in the jungle, running from the Philippine military as they sought to rescue us. On June 7, 2002, through the bravery of many men, they finally found us and rushed our encampment in an effort to rescue us. Sadly, during the skirmish, my husband Martin was shot and killed. I was seriously wounded, but was rescued and returned to my three children.

I love the song "I Believe." It puts into words many of my feelings during that year of captivity. I remember during our tenth week as hostages I had a real crisis of faith. I decided that God didn't love me. If He loved me, I would be out of there. Hadn't I begged and pleaded for Him to effect our release? This decision led to depression, anger, and my being generally miserable.

After a few days of this, Martin came to me and said, "Gracia — it is so hard for me to see you giving up your faith like this." I retorted, "I haven't given up my faith! I still believe in Almighty God and His Son, our Savior. I have just decided that He doesn't really love me." Martin's reply was, "Seems to me that you either believe it all or you don't believe it at all." I did some soul searching that day and decided that I needed to believe what was true — not believe based on how I felt. I could recall Scripture after Scripture that tells us that God loves us. And I made a decision that day — I was going to believe that what God says is true. My crisis of faith passed based on that decision.

And as this song says, "Still, it was so hard to wait!" We prayed daily for God to speed the days of our release. But as time dragged on — as we ran and hiked and starved — our faith became stronger.

It has been over two years now since Martin's death. People often greet me with the words, "You are so brave. You have such great faith!" My answer to them is, "No. My faith is very small. But when I am faithless, God is faithful." My cry to God today remains the same as that father who long ago brought his demon-possessed son to Jesus and pleaded with Him to heal him. Jesus said, "If thou canst believe, all things are possible." And the father cried, "Lord, I believe, help my unbelief!"

We all make choices every day. Let's choose to *believe* that what God says is true, and let's see what a difference it will make in our lives.

Common Bond

— Doug McKelvey and Steve Siler

Through the breaking of his body, His body we became.
How great the Father's mercy, to call us by His name.
Blood was mixed with water,
Pouring from His side
To cleanse our guilt as sinners,
To wash us as His bride.

Chorus:
Called by the love of the Father,
Sealed in the blood of the Son,
And all who respond share a common bond,
A common bond that will not come undone.

He bore our heavy burdens
And bids us do the same,
Supporting one another,
United in His name.
As members of one Body,
We are called to peace,
Finding in His perfect love a perfect unity.

One heart, one love, one Spirit,
One hope to stand upon.
One faith, one joy, one purpose,
One perfect common bond.

Common Bond

There are few joys in life like realizing you have something in common with someone else. You find out you both know someone, vacationed at the same campground, or attended the same school. It sounds so trivial, but when you're in a strange place, alone and uncomfortable, having someone who can relate to you and you to them is priceless.

In 1987, I joined my family in singing in Branson, Missouri, at the Braschler Music Show. My parents began this unique ministry in 1983 after my father served as a senior pastor for over 28 years in the church. Following our college graduations, my wife and I decided it was time to join the family business.

The schedule for the show was pretty much the same every day. Arrive early enough to usher people to their seats, change into our stage clothes, sing the first half, come down to greet people during intermission, then finish the show. Every night people would come to the platform during intermission where the performers would stand to greet and sign autographs. Invariably there would be someone, in the midst of a conversation, who knew someone you knew. It was exciting and sometimes comical to see these conversations unfold.

On one particular evening, two retired couples came up to speak to me during the intermission. The conversation began with the usual questioning about their hometown, and frequency of trips to the Branson area and our show. These two couples were from Indiana, just east of Indianapolis, an area I was born in and lived while my father pastored a church. I began asking questions about their retirement and the years before. Come to find out, one of the ladies had been an elementary school teacher in Indiana for years before retirement. When I inquired about the city, she identified Anderson, Indiana — the town I used to live in. I continued to inquire about the years she taught and what school — Franklin Elementary in the late 60s and 70s — the exact years I was in elementary at the same school. She finally inquired about my teachers. Staring at the ceiling for accurate memory I began, "Ms. Tatman in kindergarten, Ms. Gustin in first grade, Ms. Jackson in second grade, Ms. Uh. . . ." She suddenly gasped and stopped me with a shout, "I'm Ms. Jackson."

Sure enough, it was my second grade teacher from 1970 who somehow ran into me 17 years later at a music show. Suddenly, these strangers who seemed unknown and somewhat distant were hugging and kissing and crying and taking pictures with me. We held that line up for 20 minutes, laughing and catching up on our lives. It was an experience I'll never forget.

This story reminds me today of how I believe God intended the body of Christ to treat one another. In a world that is becoming more diverse in beliefs, morals, and truth, God chose a way to keep us connected by sending His Son to perish for us all. Regardless of the argument some may use to separate themselves from others who believe in God, sending His Son to die makes us familiar with each other regardless. It draws us together because of this great act of love.

What would the church be like if those of us who attended actually treated one another like brothers and sisters in Christ? Peter reminds us of this type of love with these words:

"Now that you have purified yourselves by obeying the truth so that you have sincere love for your brothers, love one another deeply, from the heart" (1 Pet. 1:22; NIV).

We are so different in so many ways in the body of Christ, only the power of God could truly draw us together in unity. This song reminds me as I sing that my dear friends, my extended family — 98 percent of whom I have no memory of or past history with are seated before me in churches where God opens the door to minister. When their hearts break, mine should break. When they are in pain, God calls me to feel the pain as well. When the world seems indifferent to their suffering, God calls me to a broken heart. He calls us to carry burdens for others, even others we don't know.

Mrs. Jackson was a stranger to me that day until I realized what we both had in common. From then on, she became one of my dearest friends. God's call is so very clear in His word: ". . . love one another deeply." Through Christ, this bond will not come undone.

Common Bond

Mark Shaner *is an ordained minister and serves as Leadership Development Director in the area of young people for the Church of God, Anderson, Indiana. His career has included many years as a pastor to youth in Florida and Kansas. Through ministry and missions trips, he has influenced hundreds of God's children around the world, not the least of which are his own: Mark and wife, Vickie, are parents to Gina, Zack, Austin, and Timothy. The family lives in Anderson, Indiana, where Vickie home schools the younger Shaner kids, while Gina attends Anderson University. Mark is a high school friend of Todd's, who also served on staff with Todd and 11 other pastors at the Central Community Church in Wichita, Kansas.*

"My prayer for all of them is that they will be one, just as you and I are one, Father — that just as you are in me and I am in you, so they will be in us, and the world will believe you sent me" (Jesus' prayer for us in John 17:21; NLT).

My parents divorced when I was ten years old. The divorce was such a surprise and shock for me. The pain that followed was intense and physical; I ended up in the hospital for two weeks with ulcers!

After the completion of the divorce, I lived with my Dad. Dad gave me tremendous freedom on the outside, but as a ten year old, I was completely torn up on the inside: my emotions were as damaged as my stomach had been, but the treatment was something I had to find for myself.

At 13, I began to attend the Tanner Street Church of God in Sikeston, Missouri. There I heard over and over again how I could be free on the inside through Jesus. I observed this church family and the love they demonstrated and quickly realized that they had something that I was missing: they had a common bond through a personal relationship with Jesus Christ.

Jesus' last prayer for us in John 17 was "that we might be one." As a freshman in high school, I remember walking an aisle and giving my life to Jesus Christ. The ulcer disappeared and new life started! I became a new creation, old things were passed away and everything became new (2 Cor. 5:17). I, too, now had this common bond!

As a high school student I visited a number of congregations in Missouri and Illinois; I attended Warner Southern College in Lake Wales, Florida; I've been to remote people groups in Panama, Honduras, Guatemala, and throughout the Caribbean. I have been to Russia, India, Bangladesh, Bhutan, and India. I have been in many situations where I did not even speak the same language or share the same culture, and yet there has always been a common bond with the people of God: We are a part of the body of Christ globally!

We have a common bond — regardless of geographical locations, denominational allegiances, gender, age, or color of skin, we are called to be one in Christ because we have responded to Christ and we share a *common bond* that will not come undone.

"Now you are the body of Christ, and each one of you is part of it" (1 Cor. 12:27).

This is the Beginning

—Twila McBride and Matthew West

Nailed to a cross, feeling his life slip away.
The sun's going down;
He's paying the cost for all of his foolish mistakes.
Who will save him now?
Guilty, but searching for mercy in Jesus' eyes,
Finding a Savior, the promise of paradise.

Chorus:
This is the beginning, this is love.
He's holding your tomorrow
And all you dreamed of.
The power of forgiveness
Will set you free.
It may look like the end but believe,
This is the beginning

Chained to this world,
Watching your strength disappear.
Shadows surround you,
Time after time changing your courage for fear.
Who can you turn to?
Empty, but searching for mercy in Jesus' eyes
You'll find the Savior, the promise of paradise.

This is the Beginning

Imagine how different the world would be if we were given the ability to see the unforeseen. To see the potential in situations or to assess the real needs of people beyond what they express would truly be a valued gift. The challenge for leaders, pastors, parents, and counselors is not just in the hearing or in the explanation of a current situation. The demand on these leadership roles requires the ability to see beyond the obvious. To think deeper, stretch imaginations further, and assess beyond the immediate and current to the possible and potential. Of all the talents to improve upon, the ability to help people see beyond today is certainly one of the greatest needs in the world today.

Imagine how different America would be if everyone could see past the current political situations to what these struggles might bring to the world. Imagine how differently we would live our lives with the clear vision and picture of the second coming of Christ. Dream about a series of relationships where you were often given opportunity to help someone see a potential future beyond the struggles of today.

This ability brings a precious gift to the receiver – perspective. With perspective, we can withstand and often conquer our fears. With perspective, the current struggle or situation seems just a part of our life – not our *entire* life. A loved one passes away – with perspective we see that death is as much a part of life as birth. We are able to place this tragedy within the context of the rest of our life, in perspective, and it fits without drowning or destroying everything else.

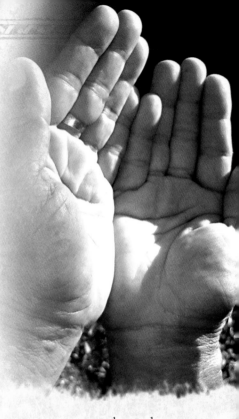

This truth is especially evident and a source of strength when our future has already been dedicated to Christ. As a pastor I often met parents who were so excited to participate in a child dedication service at church. When dedicating our children we are in essence saying, "God, however you wish to use the life of this child, I place them in Your hands." What's sad is that we then often spend the next 25 years or more worrying about our children. This seems to be a contradiction to the dedication service. Why ask God to care for our children and lead them if we plan on worrying about them for the rest of their lives? In the same way, trusting God with the future, the unforeseen, is a powerful way to worship Him in faith. We never know how God will use a current situation to bring glory to himself as well as bring tremendous blessing to us.

In 1984 my four years of college at Anderson University were coming to a close. For the past three years I had been fortunate to room or run with friends who owned vehicles. Through their generosity, I rarely went without wheels. It was also a gift to have someone from my home town to ride home with every summer and during breaks through those years. However, two weeks before the end of my senior year, I found myself without a ride back to my hometown of St. James, MO. Everyone seemed to have other plans that year, and I found myself practicing the hitchhiker maneuver, just in case.

One evening, through a conversation with a friend, I remembered a girl I had once met in high school who lived in Springfield, MO. She was finishing her senior year as well, and after a quick phone call, I had secured my ride home. Claudia Wampler was a preacher's daughter from Missouri. She and I had been acquaintances over a four-year time frame. When she came to pick me up on that warm May morning in 1984, I had no idea what God had planned.

During that ride home (and after one of my championship backrubs while she drove through St. Louis), we struck up a relationship that extended far beyond that car ride. We dated the rest of the year and into the fall, and in June of 1985 I asked Claudia to be my wife. We were married in September of 1985 and we are still celebrating.

If I could have seen far into the future the picture of the wife God wanted me to marry, how differently would I have spent those four years in preparation? I had actually given up on finding a Christian wife after four years of school and really was leaving college very defeated about my dating relationships. The desire to even date or look further for a mate had actually faded away completely. My friends and I had replaced our efforts to date with time spent working out and playing basketball. I thought I was done looking for quite a while.

When I first heard the words for the song "This is the Beginning," I misunderstood the meaning, and actually passed on the tune. I thought it was another song about the crucifixion, and that the title was referring to the beginning of Christ ruling over death. What a surprise to discover that this song was not only about the crucifixion, but that the story was about someone else — in addition to Christ!

The story of the two thieves hanging on either side of Christ is revealed in Luke 23:39-43:

One of the criminals who hung there hurled insults at him: "Aren't you the Christ? Save yourself and us!" But the other criminal rebuked him, "Don't you fear God," he said, "since you are under the same sentence? We are punished justly, for we are getting what our deeds deserve. But this man has done nothing wrong." Then he said, "Jesus, remember me when you come into your kingdom." Jesus answered him, "I tell you the truth, today you will be with me in paradise."

Can you imagine the scene in the jail cell that morning as these two thieves huddled together in a cell, knowing that this day was going to be their final day? Remembering their families and children, seeing old friends standing outside the jail cell, and imagining the horror awaiting them in the afternoon must have drowned their thoughts in sorrow and fear. At the same time, I'm sure they heard what was happening just outside their cell doors: the yelling, scourging, and beating being poured upon Jesus Christ. Then to suddenly have the doors flung open by the Centurion — they must have cried out as they were dragged from their cells, put in chains, and shoved into the street to begin the long march out of town to the Hill of Golgotha. They knew the end was near. As they made their way down the road, hearing the taunts, feeling the spit of those lining the road, they must have been tortured with the loss of hope for the remainder of this day.

And then, after what must have seemed like miles of walking and parading out of town, to be nailed to a cross and hoisted in the darkening sky toward the heavens; from that cross I'm sure the two thieves could see their own homes, places they had worked, and schools they attended as children. It was all coming to an end. Accepting death and the end of everything you know has to be a very introspective experience. I would assume that the sound of the crowd quickly faded in the minds of these men as their strength and resolve began to depart. The end was nearer.

It must have been confusing in the midst of their suffering and pending death to witness the crucifixion of Jesus Christ between them. This man seemed to garner such hatred and scorn from the crowd.

How powerful was the scene at that moment? Through the acknowledgment of the Christ, the request for forgiveness, and the promise of a home in paradise, the thief running toward his death and eternal damnation sees eternity change in an instant. Who could have imagined that this would be the end of a life seemingly lived in sin? Yet, Jesus heard him and in one sentence brought a vision and reward that I'm sure this thief never imagined possible.

This song was chosen for the *Common Bond* project with a powerful message of hope for things unseen. It's a call to dedicate the future, the unforeseen, to Christ today. In challenging people to dream with God about everything, this type of faith requires a hope beyond our belief. Romans 8:24-25 tells us:

"...But hope that is seen is no hope at all. Who hopes for what he already has? But if we hope for what we do not yet have, we wait for it patiently."

This is the beginning, not the end. I encourage you today to seek the hope of Christ for things unseen. What seems to be the end in a portion of your life can be used by God as a glorious beginning if dedicated to Him.

This is the Beginning

Dianne Coleman *is a study in perpetual motion.*
Not only is she an Assistant Dean and lecturer for the W. Frank
Barton School of Business, but she is also a mom to three sons. She
loves to crochet and she finds time to work out every day! Dianne
served on an Assimilation team with Todd and many others at
Central Community Church in Wichita.

She wore a beautiful, long white dress with lace all around, sewn by her mother's hands. A flowing, store-bought veil of white atop her brown hair made the precious seven year old truly look like a child of Jesus. It was First Communion Day and with prayer book and a new, white rosary in hand she marched down the church aisle to receive Jesus into her heart for the very first time. She loved Jesus as only a seven year old could and she said her prayers daily, especially the ones that had been carefully memorized for this special day. Five years later, this child of Jesus rededicated her life on Confirmation Day. Jesus was still in her heart and a part of her daily life.

The next year, following her graduation from the eighth grade, she left her home in Kansas for a convent in Tulsa, OK. Once again dressed in flowing white dress and veil, she marched down the church aisle giving herself totally to her bridegroom, Jesus. Two years later, with heart trembling, she was returned home for reasons she did not understand. Why was He deserting her? What was to become of her? At age 20 she tried to begin a new life on her own, still grieving at what was no longer. Her grief turned to hurt and anger and she turned to a life that was worldly, focusing on self and survival.

Wrong choices became a routine part of her life for the next ten years as she struggled to find herself and make this new life something meaningful. Despite her conviction that she could make it on her own, there was a tugging in her heart that wouldn't let her rest peacefully — it was a nagging feeling that all was not right, but she didn't know what to do.

She had a son and realized that she needed to make her relationship right with the Lord and search for a father for her son. God was good and sent a husband that was capable of providing for her and her son. All of their physical needs were met — in abundance. She grew in her career and added even more finances to the family resources. Life became more and more materialistic as both careers grew successfully and the country club scene was the only goal that was fulfilling. Life was happening, and God was not a part of it; she did not stick up for her beliefs and was weak in her faith.

Two more children were born, and she let her husband determine the environment in which their children were raised. They did not pray or read Bible stories or go to church.

How my heart is broken as I recall my life at this point. For 18 years of marriage I struggled with this loss of God in my life. I cried so many nights not knowing how to change the life pattern I was in. My marriage was not built on true love and for years the distance between my husband and I increased. God was never the center of our home or our relationship. Our marriage was destined to fail without God in it and so it ended with much anger, hatred, and bitterness. I cried and cried and cried out to God once again. I was so angry at myself: How could I have been so weak for so long? I would never be able to forgive myself for not teaching my three sons about the love of Jesus. How could I go on with such guilt and sorrow? I ate to soothe the depression; in three years I gained 50 pounds.

One day I found myself sitting in the parking lot of Central Community Church. I don't know how I got there — it was not on my normal driving route to and from work. I wandered inside and pulled some brochures from the racks. (I am convinced now that God had finally had enough of my behavior and intervened in a dramatic way!) I read the information and somehow the next Sunday morning I found myself at the doorway to a Sunday school class that appeared to have an attendance of nearly 100. I felt the urge to leave — I was not like these people! This was not for me! Before I could escape, a wonderful lady put her arm around my shoulders and asked, "Is this your first time here?" As I whispered yes, she turned me around and said, "Let me introduce you to some other ladies here." She was God's angel sent to touch me that day and what wonderful friends God brought to me through this class.

Throughout the next year I attended a Divorce Recovery Support Group at the church, and I slowly began to heal. But God was not finished.

The following year He brought Pastor Todd Braschler into my life. Todd asked me to join his new ministry team. I was still hurting and I told Todd that I would not be good for the team. I will never forget his prayer for me that day as he quoted Psalm 37:4, "Delight yourself in the Lord and he will give you the desires of your heart." How could I ever be worthy to receive any desires of my heart after the last 30 years of mistakes?

I had not yet heard the song "This Is The Beginning," but this song exactly expresses my feelings at that moment as I recall it now! "The sun's going down; I'm paying for all of my foolish mistakes. Who will save me now? Guilty, but searching for mercy in Jesus' eyes."

Pastor Todd insisted. I came to understand that my life and my gifts were not for my benefit, but for the Lord's, and I needed to refocus my life from self-pity to heavenly service. It took nearly two years of prayer, rededication, and hard work, but I finally fell in total submission to God's will for my life. And He is fulfilling His promise to grant me the desires of my heart as I find total delight in His presence in my life. I have been blessed with the strength to put my life back in order emotionally, physically, and spiritually — and blessed as well with my three incredible sons, church friends, and supportive family.

We have such an awesome God — He is my God of third and fourth and fifth chances. He never deserted me; I turned my back on Him. I'm still growing and healing but the pain is less and the joys are greater. I struggle with guilt and pray my sons will one day know the Jesus that I know and love. I trust He will one day touch their lives and bring them close to Him — that is the final desire of my heart and I know He will honor that desire. So, "this is the beginning, this is love. He's holding my tomorrow and all I dreamed of. The power of forgiveness will set me free. It may look like the end, but I do believe — this is the beginning!"

Forgiven

— Steve Siler and Scott Krippayne

Your grace is a mystery,
It amazes me every time
And the patience you have with me
Sees beyond all my alibis
If you had built a barrier
Then I'd understand
But you draw me closer.
With the guidance of your gentle hands

Chorus:
Yeah, yeah, yeah I'm forgiven,
I'm forgiven, you set me free
Yeah, yeah, yeah I'm forgiven,
I'm forgiven, you've forgiven me

There's no way I can comprehend
How you discipline with such love
Everyday, I fall short again
But if I repent, it's enough
You could have kept your distance and criticized
Instead you wash away my sin
In the river of your sacrifice

There's nothing I can do to be worthy
Of your mercy that you give
But still you reached out to save me
And bring new life again

Forgiven

In God's great wisdom, He allowed my parents to raise four children, of which I am the oldest. My youngest brother was born less than five years behind me. So you can imagine the battles and struggles that took place on any given day in the back seat of the multitude of station wagons and vans in our family. In an effort to keep the peace, my father laid down the law on fighting and bickering in the car early on; if anyone was caught in an argument or found tormenting someone else, my dad would turn around and look at us in the back seat (while driving 70 miles an hour) and force the offenders to slide over next to that person and ride down the road hugging one another. It was sheer torture. The person you were just fighting with was now, for as long as it took, all but sitting in your lap. I can still remember hugging my sister and bawling my eyes out in disgust at such a despicable request.

It didn't take us long to figure out that regardless of how wrong the other person was, forgiveness was golden compared to hugging them. It wasn't until high school that I realized how difficult it had become for any of us to

hold a grudge against one another. We had been taught to instantly forgive and forget.

This song was included in our list because of its foundational message to the individual and to the church. In an effort to sing to the church about the "church God dreams about," I soon realized that there are barriers to people seeing the church and themselves the way God sees them. Many of those barriers have to do with difficult church situations, betrayals by leaders, and decisions to hold onto hurt feelings thinking it is somehow punishing the offender. In order to approach this subject later in our concerts, I felt we had to provide a worship experience where people heard themselves singing these words.

I sing this song with three groups of people in mind.

1. Those who have known the Lord for many years. I use these words as a reminder of God's grace during the time in our lives when we did not know how God would use us, and yet He did. I pray for God's refreshment to those who have served Him faithfully and have preserved a tender heart for those who have never known Him.

2. Those who have recently accepted Christ, and are now looking for a way to invest their life for Him. The phrase in the song "there's nothing I could do to be worthy of the mercy that You give," takes me back to a time early in my personal walk when I was trying so desperately to earn God's grace, only to realize that it was free to me. A large portion of the "peace of God" comes as a new believer when I learn to rest in what God has done for me, and commit to find a ministry to give myself to that provides that same opportunity for others.

3. Those who have yet to make that commitment of salvation a part of their life. I think of my ugly past and the memories that accompany these thoughts as a backpack of bricks. They are heavy, cumbersome bricks from my past that are often used to define me *by my past*. My prayer in including this song is to paint a different picture for someone — perhaps you — of an existence without the backpack. Imagine a new definition of you over and above the past.

"Therefore we do not lose heart. Though outwardly we are wasting away, yet inwardly we are being renewed day by day. For our light and momentary troubles are achieving for us an eternal glory that far outweighs them all. So we fix our eyes not on what is seen, but on what is unseen. For what is seen is temporary, but what is unseen is eternal."
II Corinthians 4:16-18

Forgiven

Jeff and Kim Jones *have devoted themselves to God's service. They have taught Sunday school classes, led youth groups, and served on various ministry teams. Jeff served for several years as a minister in churches in Kansas and Arkansas. They now live in Kansas where Jeff spends his daytime hours as VP of a commercial construction group and Kim works in marketing. They are the proud parents of sons Cory, who is in the United States Navy, and Josh, a recent high school graduate. Jeff and Kim became acquainted with Todd through ministry at Central Community Church.*

I was raised in a great home, but like so many families, ours fell apart as my parents divorced. I had just entered my teenage years and, suddenly without a family structure, I didn't see much wrong in a little experimentation with drugs. I had easy access to about anything I wanted. I was without boundaries in the actions I pursued and the risks I took. Often, at the age of 13, I would sneak out of my house and just wander. At first I did this on my bike, but eventually I would just steal a car from one of my family members. Once I even totaled my sister's car in an accident with two other vehicles.

The next few years brought more excess. I moved from one parent's home to the other and back; I tried more drugs. By the time I was 15 I'd begun dealing to my friends. One of my close friends died of an overdose, but it didn't affect me the way it should have.

At 17 I drove 200 miles to Kansas City: I was drunk and stoned the entire trip. During my visit I stole something from a store with video surveillance; I was arrested and spent the weekend in juvenile detention until the authorities were able to contact my parents — who had no idea I was in Kansas City.

I also played in a rock band during those years. I can remember partying our proceeds away in hotel rooms where we'd consume any amount of drugs and booze we could get our hands on—which was plenty!

My renegade lifestyle continued through high school — though I somehow managed to graduate — and beyond. In June of 1977 I met Kim — we were both 17 and we had an instant connection. We did everything together: drugs, sex, and rock-n-roll! Within a year we were married and our wild lifestyle didn't change for five years.

Then my sister began attending church. While I was quite cynical of church and people who called themselves Christians, I couldn't deny that there was something good happening to my sister — and she and her husband had been co-partiers and best friends with Kim and me for years. After nearly a year's worth of attempts on my sister's part to get us to attend, we finally agreed to visit her church for "family day." I had really only attended to get her to quit asking me!

But something in that church wouldn't leave us. It wasn't instant — that first day we smoked a joint as soon as we got out of the parking lot! But eventually we began attending more. There was something there that I didn't understand at all, and it drew me back. Finally, in April of 1983, my wife and I went to the altar and asked God to forgive our sins. We gave our lives to God. I learned the power of God's forgiveness that day!

I've left many details out in the telling of my life before Christ — tragedies and regrets that many others have experienced as well. But it is enough to tell you that I was delivered from a life of sin by a God that is able. I wish I could say that in the 20 years that I have been a Christian I have gotten this "Christian Life" thing all figured out. But I don't.

I quit my job and went into full-time ministry and what I can say, what I understand best is that I walk in grace from God. I walk knowing "if we confess our sins, He is faithful and just to forgive our sins and to cleanse us from all unrighteousness." (I John vs. 1:9). I walk knowing that the first part of my life definitely needed God's forgiveness and the part I am living now needs God's forgiveness — not so much for the things I have done, but for the things that I haven't.

Listening to "Forgiven" reminds me that being forgiven is a gift from God that comes with such joy! And it reminds me of the need to live life with the confidence of knowing that.

Worthy After All

— Todd Braschler, Tony Elenberg, Todd Laffoon

In my younger days I dreamed
Of how my life would be
Something even better than
My family gave to me
God was working in my heart
So how could I fall
His strength made perfect through me
As I answered his call

But that's not how life happened
As I've come to see
For though I tried to live my dream
I met reality
The dream I held was not to be,
I set myself aside
Then Jesus came and drew me in
He turned to me and cried

Chorus:
Worthy after all, all the shattered
dreams
That always seem to hold you down
Worthy after all, all the bitter shame
Of yesterday that held you bound
Worthy after all

Even though the haunting memories
still come around
When you know Me, you'll know My
heart
Then you'll see yourself,
Worthy after all

Knowing life is less than what it ought
to be
Is only the beginning to see life as He
sees
I see all the failure
But God sees the rest
When I see nothing but the worst
He sees all the best

Worthy to serve Me
Worthy to love Me
Worthy to receive My all
You are worthy of honor
And worthy of forgiveness
You are worthy of a higher call

Worthy After All

The Incredible Hulk was one of my favorite shows growing up as a kid. In those days, Lou Ferrigno was about the coolest guy on TV. The story plots were always similar: The Hulk's alter-ego, Bruce Banner, seemed mild and kind until you ticked him off. Then suddenly, his clothes ceased to fit. He would quickly double in size, turn green, and save whatever part of the world he happened to have wandered into. It could happen! I once knew a teacher who…. never mind.

Every week there was a phrase that Bruce Banner used to end every episode and as a committed "hulk-maniac," I always watched the entire show to hear these eternal words: *Don't make me mad! You won't like me when I'm mad!*

I guess I didn't really understand the impact of that phrase on my life until my first few years of college. As most college students did, I often found myself testing God and pushing my limits of right and not-so-right. I can sadly remember a few times when I thought I had blown it with God. A lack of commitment to attending church, creating habits and attitudes that were not pleasing to Him, and questioning just about everything I had been taught seemed to be my greatest challenges. These were the times when I was sure God was standing up in heaven in a shredded white robe turning green with anger, preparing to leap down and squish me. If God had gone "Hulky" on me at the time I would have deserved it. Instead, a strange thing happened: I realized for the first time that God was not Bruce Banner. I mean, Bruce Banner-like. He wasn't up there waiting for me to mess up everything so He could muster His strength and crush me. In fact, something even more impressive and powerful happened. It didn't just happen once, it happened time and time again. God continued to forgive. He didn't just forgive, however. He seemed to lavish me with His love so powerfully that it caused a change in me. I couldn't seem to run Him off. He didn't squish me and vanquish me from His presence like I thought He would. In my case, God didn't win me over because of a great healing or a great deliverance from substance abuse or by a startling transformation. He simply overwhelmed me with grace. He taught me that condemnation ended with His death, and grace powerfully began at His resurrection. He helped me see that the feelings of inadequacy and shame did not come from Him. Therefore, He helped me recognize those feelings as they had originated from outside of heaven.

After serving as a pastor following those tumultuous years, I began to meet hundreds and hundreds of people in and out of the church who still believed the lie I could so easily recall hearing. "You're not worthy! God can't use you. You're damaged goods." I found people, some who even knew Christ personally, continuing to place themselves in a secret place in the church. I call it the "scratch and dent section of the church." This is a special place reserved for those of us who sense that our life may not be as pure as those around us. Sometimes we placed ourselves there, other times the church escorted us to this section.

I've found this section to be quite obvious in every church. It's filled with those who feel unworthy of a call from God on their lives because of their past. Some believed that God had a dream for them at one time, but who now have a skewed perception of God, thinking He is too ashamed of them to follow through with His dream.

This song was my first attempt at writing music for anyone to listen to. It came through conversations with my dear friend, Todd Laffoon, and is based on a portion of his life as a young Christian struggling to mature. The chorus was written in June of 2001 in a basement studio with my close friend, Tony Elenburg, just outside of Nashville, TN. Todd Laffoon and I had taken a weekend to visit Tony to gain his wisdom on this whole Christian artist dream. God's dream for me.

The first and second verses and the bridge were written on a white marker board while writing alone in my Sunday school classroom later that summer at Central Community Church in Wichita, KS. This entire song was not only inspired by Todd's testimony; these words seemed to minister deeply into my own experience. I also felt that God was leading all of us to speak to the "scratch and dent" section in churches. As a group writing this song, we felt that in order for churches to mature into the "church God dreams about," individual people had to define themselves through the eyes of Christ rather than by their past.

My prayer in choosing and writing this song for *Common Bond* was to move my concerts from a corporate praise-and-worship experience, to a time when God might bring tremendous healing in the lives of His children. I pray God answers those prayers in your life as you listen.

Worthy After All

Todd Laffoon

never imagined himself living in Wichita, KS in a home completely outnumbered by females. But he seems to kind of enjoy it — although he is quick to remind you that he grew up in Norman, OK where he attended the University of Oklahoma and played in "The Pride of Oklahoma Marching Band." When not at work as a self-described tech-junkie (really, Director of Sales and Marketing for an electronic data storage company), he still enjoys playing his trumpet in church and community bands. A licensed pilot, he loves to fly but will choose a vacation scuba diving with his family (wife Jill and daughters Jessi and Sami) over any other activity. Todd Laffoon is not only a dear friend of Todd Braschler's, but he is also the President of Todd Braschler Ministries.

We live in a world (and especially a nation) of "scorekeepers". Everyone keeps score in multiple ways: Sports teams amount to nothing if they don't rank highly — and coaches are fired for not taking their teams to number one. Marketers program us to keep score by what we do and do not have. Some individuals and corporations alike keep score by career status. All of us have kept score by the amount of money we've earned or saved or spent. The attitude of "the one who dies with the most toys wins" is everywhere. Scorekeeping is so prevalent that we even tend to grade or score crimes… and then we sometimes grade sins, too.

Sometimes scorekeeping can be in terms of negatives: Someone (you) might say, "I don't have the skills for that" or "I'll never be able to afford that." I think a lot of us tend to let that scorekeeping mentality spill over into our spiritual life and we start keeping score there. Some people give themselves points by inflating their ego… "I've done all the right works so God must be pleased with me!" While others forfeit the game by holding themselves back from service because of a bad "record."

I think this is all part of Satan's battle plan against people. First, he gets us used to keeping records and scorecards on everything, and then he goes to work on our conscience by telling us that our record of past sins disqualifies us from service. Of course, this is not God's way.

I lost sight of the fact that God does not keep score — that He in fact takes confessed sins and separates them from His followers as far as the east is from the west. I was lucky. Someone else saw me taking myself out of the game, and reminded me of the truth.

It was the spring of 2000 and I had signed up to participate in a Men's Golf Retreat with my church. My wife and I had been attending services there for more than a year, but we'd just started attending Sunday school and I thought the golf trip would be a good way to get to know some of the guys from my class. Plus, it was in Texas and the thought of four days golfing in the sun was pretty appealing in itself! I was assigned to share a room with one of the pastors on staff — Todd Braschler. (I found out later that he'd rigged the room assignments. He had an agenda.)

So there we were in Texas. It was not quite the trip we'd expected. The 70 degree days we'd envisioned turned out to be in the high 30s. The pro shop was sold out of sweatshirts within 30 minutes and a few of us with two right hand gloves had turned one inside out so that it would fit our opposite hand and ward off frostbite. The first afternoon it was so cold that we went back to the room to thaw out. Upon arriving at our room, Todd Braschler confronted me by bluntly asking me why I wasn't involved more in our church in terms of serving other people.

I told him the problem was that my past was not what he might think it was. To just meet me, as Todd had, my life looked like a pretty picture: I grew up in a Christian home, had great Christian friends that had been close to me since childhood. My beautiful wife was my best friend and we loved our two great daughters. I was blessed with a good career and a nice house…I was a pretty happy guy. But the truly ugly part that I did not like to discuss fell between my life as a child and my life today. Since graduating from college I'd had two failed marriages that, added together, did not total more than 14 months. I had made mistakes that had left scars on my record and based on this, I disqualified myself from serving God — even though my college years had been filled with happy service in the church. Since then, though, well, I felt like I just had too low of a score in God's eyes.

To his credit, Todd didn't call me an idiot straight out. He patiently led me through a rediscovery of James 1:2 (pure joy through trials of many kinds). That conversation with Todd was a turning point in my life. When we returned from the golf trip I took the leap and started serving. I found great new friends… and I found that you always find the best friends when you serve with them.

I began to use my gifts of leadership, teaching Sunday school on occasion and taking on a role in the leadership team of the class. Eventually I even reclaimed a long retired gift of music and began playing trumpet in the church orchestra. When Todd was ready to take his own leap into a new ministry, I was glad to be a part of it.

One of our first planning meetings was in Nashville, TN with Tony Elenberg, an old friend of Todd's who has spent years as a Christian recording artist and offered to coach us a little on some of the practical points of such a ministry. As we discussed the ministry, Tony asked me how I had come to know Todd. I told him the story of the golf trip and that we felt strongly that the goal of our ministry would include encouraging others to reclaim their gifts and use them for the Lord, regardless of their history. And that is how we began to write this song, "Worthy After All."

Throughout our discussion, words like "shame" and "disqualified" kept coming up, along with phrases that described a sense that you weren't where you thought you'd end up — that the life you'd strived for was shattered by your past. Then we tried to envision what God would say to this line of thinking: He'd say, "You are worthy after all to serve!"

And so, I found myself part of a Christian song writing team! More than that, I am a small part of a ministry that is all about helping God's people through tough times like I experienced because I had scored myself too low.

Maybe that's where you are — I think it's a common place to be. You may not be ready to serve because you feel you're not worthy. Or maybe you don't know Christ and are waiting to trust Him and Him to trust you. But here is the truth: we are all sinners and God doesn't score our sins. He offers us gifts and waits for us to use them. Serving has healed my heart, and it is my prayer that my story, our song, and God's grace will lead you to trust Him to heal your heart as well.

I Am Holding You

—Benjamin Gaither, Suzanne Jennings, and John Piscotta

When you soar on eagle's wings
Or make your bed beneath the seas
Darkness will be light to me
I am holding you

In spite of what you think you are
And your tendency to work too hard
You can never run too far
I am holding you

And my heart will take you home
And my hand will lead you on

Even when you doubt my plan
When you fail to understand
You can touch my nail-scarred hands
I am holding you

I knew you in my secret place
And I cannot forget your face
So lay back in my saving grace
I am holding you
I am holding you
I am holding you
I am holding you

I Am Holding You

Of all the Bible characters there are to identify with, Peter has to be one I most relate to. My dad used to say my mouth was always two sentences ahead of my brain. Like Peter, you never had to wonder about any thoughts I was having because they very often arrived into the open before I had a chance to think them through. Peter seems to have been possessed with this same disease as well. Not only can I relate to the boldness and lack of control Peter displayed at times, I too nearly lost my life underwater.

My father's side of the family is from the southeast corner of Missouri. He was raised on the Current River in Doniphon, MO, so usually once a year our family made the trek to the Ozarks to create great memories on the river. The Current River didn't receive its name because it stands still. Whirlpools and strong undercurrents greet you around every bend on a float trip from Deer Lodge to the Arkansas state line.

Our family get-togethers always included cousins, aunts, uncles, a hay wagon, plenty of watermelon, and a gravel bar. When we wanted to swim, our folks would plunge long sticks into the gravel bar to mark the drop offs and give us strict instructions not to violate the set boundaries. Of course, we rarely paid attention to rules or boundaries after play began.

On one such occasion, one of my cousins and I drifted too far down-stream while throwing rocks together. Without warning, we both stepped into a hole that plunged our five-year-old bodies into the fast undercurrent and down the river. I can still see my cousin flailing underneath a blue sky of water, trying to regain footing and swim to the top. We were grasping for each other and trying to maneuver ourselves to the surface. Our stature together wouldn't have been enough to reach the top and a gulp of much needed air.

Suddenly, like a pelican diving for a pinfish, my cousin's father, Harrison, plunged from the sky down to the gravel bottom where we struggled. I couldn't believe it. Harrison wasn't much taller than we were, but I guess farming for most of his life gave him the strength we certainly lacked. In what seemed like a single grasp, Harrison grabbed me first, then his son, and together pulled us both to the surface. Air never felt so good.

To this day, there are many mentor relationships that mean the world to me. None, however, mean quite as much to me as my love and thankfulness for Mr. Harrison Wells. Thus, my second similarity with our friend, Peter.

He, too, disobeyed instructions from His father, stepped into a deep unknown, sensed the end of his life, and was saved by someone much stronger and wiser. Matthew 14:22-36 tells us the story of how Jesus was walking on water and Peter decided to join Him.

Immediately Jesus made the disciples get into the boat and go on ahead of him to the other side, while he dismissed the crowd. After he had dismissed them, he went up on the mountainside by himself to pray. When evening came, he was there alone, but the boat was already a considerable distance from land, buffeted by the waves because the wind was against it.

During the fourth watch of the night Jesus went out to them, walking on the lake. When the disciples saw him walking on the lake, they were terrified. "It's a ghost" they said, and cried out in fear. But Jesus immediately said to them, "Take courage! It is I. Don't be afraid." "Lord, if it's you," Peter replied, "tell me to come to you on the water." "Come," he said.

Then Peter got down out of the boat, walked on the water and came toward Jesus. But when he saw the wind, he was afraid and, beginning to sink, cried out, "Lord, save me!" Immediately Jesus reached out his hand and caught him. "You of little faith," he said, "why did you doubt."

And when they climbed into the boat, the wind died down. Then those who were in the boat worshiped him, saying, "Truly you are the Son of God" (NIV).

"I Am Holding You" was included in this recording project because we all find ourselves sinking at times.

The sense that we are lost, maybe even struggling to breathe, is not a mystery in the eyes of God. A large portion of my love for God comes from a great memory of where I was before I met Him. It comes also from a memory of the times when I was one decision away from losing it all. I'm finding it is not always just the love of God that draws me nearer to Him. It is often the imagination of what life would be like without God in my life. It's the past memories of decisions and actions that seemed to separate me from the presence of God. I thank God for His promise that "... nothing shall separate me from the love of God" (Matt. 8:35-39).

He is holding me, and He is holding you.

I Am Holding You

Few people sparkle like Koni Manzi. *Whether she is talking about her kids (Ashlie, Apryl, and Quentin), laughing at her husband's jokes, or doing dishes at a church function: she sparkles. And when she smiles at you, it is like receiving a present.*

She lives in Wichita, KS with her childhood sweetheart, Troy. Together she and Troy work in a family business and try to balance that commitment with their commitment to God and their children. Koni and Troy have been friends of Todd Braschler for the past 6 years, and attended his Sunday school class for three years at Central Community Church in Wichita.

In Deut. 31:6, it says, "Be strong and courageous, do not be afraid or terrified because of them, for the Lord your God goes with you. He will never leave nor forsake you."

I was born in Seoul, South Korea, and lived there with my mother, father, an older brother, and a sister. I also had a grandmother who would feed me apples by scooping the apples with a spoon — like apple sauce. I knew we were very poor. Our home was a four-wall shack. We didn't have a kitchen or bedrooms; the floor and a blanket served as our bed. We used a large coffee can placed in the corner as our toilet. We didn't have traditional doors with locks. I remember being left alone with the screen door secured with a chain.

One day my mother dressed me up in my best dress and took me to the market. As we walked, she kept telling me to hold tight to her hand, so I did. It was crowded and busy when we arrived at the market. My mother walked me into the center, let go of my hand and walked away. I was around three when she abandoned me.

I remember crying and running through the legs of all of the people, looking for that familiar pair of legs. But I never found her. I stayed near the market, hoping she would come back, but she didn't. I slept in a phone booth; I had nothing to eat or drink. No one noticed me or cared. It was several days before an American soldier found me and took me to a nearby orphanage.

At the orphanage they took my dress and replaced it with rags. It is possible, too, that they gave me a new name and birth date. There were so many children there like me, abandoned and forgotten. To the workers I was just one more child to feed and look after. There wasn't time for hugs or kisses, but I do recall one time when someone noticed me: I had hurt my hand and was taken into the city to see the doctor. After he bandaged me, he kissed me on the cheek. It took me by surprise. Korean men were not affectionate, but he showed me a tenderness I'll never forget.

Once in a while missionaries would come. They brought candy and pretty clothes (I'm sure they also brought useful things like paper, pencils, etc.). There was a lot of excitement as we tried the clothing on, but as soon as the missionaries left, the clothes were taken off of us and put away. We never saw them again. Most likely, they were sold.

There is a Disney movie called *The Rescuers*. One of the characters is a little girl who lives in an orphanage. She desperately wants a family of her own. In one scene, she is relating her day to a sympathetic cat. She tells how all the kids line up, so that prospective parents could look them over. She put on her best smile and prayed they would pick her. Her face fell as she told the cat they chose another girl instead. When I watched this movie, years after my orphanage experience, I could feel the pressure building in my chest until the tears finally fell: I remembered doing the same thing. I would stand there with my prettiest smile, hoping that my mother would come back or that someone would look at me and say, "We want her!"

Finally, I was chosen. Paperwork was started to complete the adoption — I was on my way to having a family. But I got sick, so sick that they didn't think I would live. The adoption was stopped and the couple chose another child. I survived the illness, but still had no family.

God is good in all things. He knew that I was not meant to be with the other couple. He already had parents picked out for me: American parents from Kansas. This couple had two sons who were grown and had started their own families. The couple wanted daughters, so they adopted one. Their new daughter needed a sister

to play with and grow up with. They began to pray that God would help them find a little girl who would grow up with the child they had adopted — so the girls would be sisters and friends.

They went back to the adoption agency that had placed their daughter with them and asked about adopting another Korean girl to be their daughter's little sister. Because the adoptive mother was in her fifties, the agency initially told them that she was too old to request a younger child. But the couple persisted and the agency finally relented and offered them a girl just under the age requirement. When they looked at the photo the agency had of the child, they fell in love. In the photo the little girl's hair is shaved off to discourage lice; she looks unkempt. The woman didn't see any of the imperfections; she saw a little girl she could love, a little girl who needed her love.

Of course, I was that girl and I've wondered many times what my mother saw in that picture she showed me years later, and so proudly displayed to others. I used to cringe — but I am thankful she saw me through our Father's eyes.

On January 21, 1974, I was put on a plane to fly across the continent. When the plane landed at Kansas City International Airport, I was placed in my new mother's arms. I was six years and three months old. I stood three feet tall and weighed 35 pounds; I was the height and weight of an average-three-year old. God was watching over me.

A couple of years after my arrival, a retired veteran approached my mother, blessing her for adopting my sister and me. He told us that Korean orphanages were so crowded that children over six were put out on the street to fend for themselves. For girls, that meant prostitution or black market slavery.

My transition to an American family confused me. I had major culture shock and I was filled with anger and hatred for my Korean mother. I colored pictures in black. My mother would tell me that my Korean mother must have loved me very much to give me up in hopes that I would have a better future. It took the gentle love and patience of my new mother to help me learn to forgive and let go — to learn that there were more colors in the rainbow to color with.

Four years after my arrival, my new parents divorced. I thought it was my fault because I wasn't my father's blood child. The following year, my grandmother passed away. I had a hard time accepting these losses. It seemed like all the people I loved left me.

God is good. He never leaves us nor forsakes us. A few years later my mom met a wonderful man — a man that had been my grandmother's Sunday school teacher! He and my mother married and he adopted my sister and me. How many people can say they were chosen, not once — but twice?

I am very close to my parents. Only a mirror shows that we are not biologically connected. What is in our hearts is much stronger. I feel special because they chose me — I love them because God gave them to me.

I am now married to my childhood sweetheart. There was a time when I wanted nothing to do with him, but God had put into his heart that I was to be his wife. With much tenacity and prayer he won my love. We have two beautiful daughters and a precocious son. Our marriage has had its ups and downs, but it is strong because we invited God to be the center of it.

God was with me on the streets of Korea. He heard my prayers while I lined up at the orphanage. He has blessed me to overflowing and still he continues to bless me. At the times of crisis in my younger life I felt abandoned and unloved. Looking back I can see that I was never alone. God was holding me in His arms.

I Sing

— Jason Hinkle

I sing to the Lord above
Who has captured my heart
With His miraculous love

I sing to the Lord on high
Who has saved my soul
And now I testify

I sing to the Lord of all
Who has heard my cry
Every time that I call

I sing to the Lord of hosts
Who is the three in one
Father, Son and Holy Ghost

Chorus:
And I will worship,
Worship you alone
You alone are the Lord of all
And my eternal home
And I will worship,
Worship you alone
You alone are the Lord of all
And my eternal home

I Sing

Every movement from God on our behalf compels a response back to Him. The day He came into your life; the moment you realized His healing in your body; the day you witnessed a miracle in the life of another. In His elaborate passion for man, God overwhelms us with His miraculous love. We sensed it before we actually knew Him, and it drew us to those who already did. We feel His presence so powerfully in our life after we make a commitment to Him. The more of our heart in His possession, the more we want to be like Him. That alone draws us to the deepest passion in the heart of God: the desire for others to become children of God as a result of our life's testimony.

"I Sing" was written by a music pastor friend, Jason Hinkle who now pastors in Bellingham, WA. Its inclusion as one of the ten songs was due to its honest and simple proclamation of **joy**. There are so many commandments in Scripture that direct and lead us to think and act in the image of God. I think God likes to hear us respond verbally to these commands from time to time, to acknowledge their truth in our life. I believe it brings great joy to the heart of God to hear us accept the challenge these Scriptures bring to us by stating these truths in prayer and in song.

The following verses come to mind when I put my voice with the heart of Pastor Jason as he was writing these words.

The priests then withdrew from the Holy Place. All the priests who were there had consecrated themselves, regardless of their divisions. All the Levites who were musicians — Asaph, Heman, Jeduthun and their sons and relatives — stood on the east side of the altar, dressed in fine linen and playing cymbals, harps and lyres. They were accompanied by 120 priests sounding trumpets. The trumpeters and singers joined in unison, as with one voice to give praise and thanks to the Lord. Accompanied by trumpets, cymbals and other instruments, they raised their voices in praise to the Lord and sang; 'He is good; his love endures forever.' Then the temple of the Lord was filled with a cloud, and the priests could not perform their service because of the cloud, for the glory of the Lord filled the temple of God (II Chron. 5:11–14).

When we sense God in this way, our hearts are completely captured by His love. Our memory engages to help us remember all that God has done for us.

"And God spoke all these words: I am the Lord your God, who brought you out of Egypt, out of the land of slavery. You shall have no other gods before me" (Exod. 20:1–3).

May this project, our praises coupled with your praises, be pleasing to Christ. We have been captured by His miraculous love. I sing only to the Lord above.

I Sing

Jill Laffoon *is many things that she thought she would never be: she is (still) a Kansan, a mother, a wife, a runner, and a scuba diver. She'll tell you that if you'd asked her as a teenager, she would have rejected all of these possibilities as ridiculous: she planned to leave her home state as soon as possible — and the idea of parenthood or marriage was not in her original plan. As far as running or diving — the failing grade she received in 10th grade P.E. should answer that pretty clearly. Nevertheless, she is all of these things — and weirdly happy about it. She lives in Wichita with her husband and best friend, Todd; daughters Jessica and Samantha; and a three-colored dog named Lucy. Todd and Jill Laffoon became acquainted with Todd Braschler through serving together in a Sunday school class at Central Community Church in Wichita. Jill serves as the ministry coordinator for Todd Braschler Ministries.*

"But let all who take refuge in you be glad; let them ever sing for joy. Spread your protection over them that those who love your name may rejoice in you." Ps 5:11

I love that line, "let them ever sing for joy." And I love this song, "I SING."

I lived a childhood filled with joy. Those who know me might find that to be a shocking statement: my childhood is not one that anyone would choose. My parents divorced when I was young. I lived with my father, who had myasthenia gravits (a form of muscular dystrophy) and diabetes — a fatal combination that stole his life slowly and with cruelty. My mother, overcome by the illness in my father, left us fighting personal battles of her own. My siblings, both much older than I, also left; my brother to college and my sister to points unknown for a while as she struggled to understand what had happened to our family. But here is the key, even as dysfunctional as we were, each of us had been saved; we knew Jesus whether we chose to acknowledge Him or not. Joy is not happiness. You can be in the worst circumstances — say dying — and not be happy about it, but still find joy.

My father, since he was legally disabled and did not work, had a legion of friends (most much older than he) that were either disabled themselves or retired or both. They called and visited and would meet my dad for lunch or breakfast or coffee. They became my friends too, teasing me, telling me jokes, and making ominous predictions about my future dates — the kinds of things old people tell ten-year-olds.

And we had a church family. Truthfully, I thought of these people more as solely my father's friends, resisting his example of faith in the midst of tragedy. But they were good to us. And I understood, even then, that despite his illness, my father had something special about him that other people wanted to be around.

It was *Joy*. He found joy in everything. From really, really bad jokes that he loved to tell, to making colored pancakes for me, to his nightly bowl of popcorn. My mother, too, could find joy, although for her it was usually found in circumstances that removed her from everyday life. She would take me to music theater and as we both became caught up in the action and the music, she'd look at me and I would look back and both of us would be smiling. For my mom, joy came in tiny flashes that surprised her I think — but she shared.

When my father died I was 16. He was 43. I was so angry. Angry at God, at all of the people who couldn't change the fact that my Dad was gone. I was angry at everyone and no one and myself. And I made stupid mistakes. I hurt people who cared for me, and I fought God.

I don't remember much joy for a while after that. But I still remembered what it felt like, and so when my first daughter was born, I recognized the feeling. I began to find it a little more often. And even as my first marriage self destructed, I found joy in my children — as God must find in his.

Finally, after a 15-year hiatus and many regrets, I returned to church. Joy was there. I met my husband Todd; a man who finds joy in loving me and the two girls he proudly calls his daughters. We are a family that laughs and fights and goes to church and makes mistakes and finds joy together and by ourselves.

I love this song for simple and selfish reasons.

When I hear "I SING," my heart beats faster and I can't help but smile. In fact, I can't help but sing. I sing for all of the times that God heard *my* call, and for all of the times that I didn't call, but He saved me anyway. He has captured my heart with His miraculous love. I have fallen on my face so many times — and still, He picked me up. I have been overwhelmed and He has pulled me through.

Todd & Nichole Smith – (Selah), Shelly Harris and Brent
Henderson singing back up vocals

One of two recording studios used in Nashville

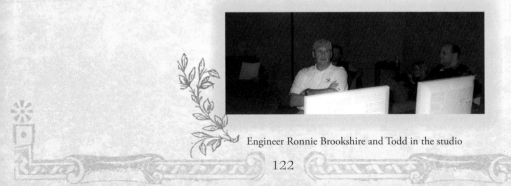

Engineer Ronnie Brookshire and Todd in the studio

Mark Pay, producer (right side)

Todd in concert; Wichita, KS

Our second studio

Sound Stage Studio J

Todd Braschler has served as a Christian artist for the past three years, singing in churches of every denomination and style of worship. Prior to this ministry, Todd served as a full-time pastor in a combination of ministries in music, youth, and assimilation/lay ministry development. In 17 years, Todd served congregations ranging from 160 to 4,000 people in Springfield, MO, West Palm Beach, FL, Lexington, KY, Casper, WY, and Wichita, KS.

In addition to his singing career, Todd also is quickly becoming an author and conference speaker for many congregations and gatherings for pastors. His "Building the Church of His Dreams" conference has been presented in a number of churches so far with very positive responses. He has a tremendous passion for the church, and his music and message both are meant to bring great encouragement to leaders and challenge to the Body of Christ. For more information about Todd Braschler Ministries, or to check our ministry schedule, go to www.toddbraschlerministires.com.

Todd has been privileged as well to be a part of a Christian hunting and fishing show based in Wichita, KS called "Diamond Adventures." You can check out more about this ministry at www.dimondadventures.com.

Finally, it's been a privilege for Todd to be involved in businesses owned or managed by Christian men and women. In an effort to help businesses align their company with the heart of God, Todd has been a part of watching Christian leaders gain greater fulfillment in business through his vision for a God-honoring company.

Jill Laffoon *serves this ministry in so many ways. In addition to working as a freelance writer, she also is very gifted in marketing and advertising as a real estate agent. Jill and her husband Todd were key in helping Todd Braschler begin this new ministry adventure. She continues to serve our ministry.*

11524 W. Ryan Circle
Wichita, KS 67205
316-729-0223 / 800-514-6775
tbraschler@cox.net
www.toddbraschlerministries.com

We would love to hear from you.

Common Bond

1. One Day *3:19*
2. God Is A Dreamer *3:31*
3. Let It Rain *4:21*
4. I Believe *3:47*
5. Common Bond *4:38*
6. This is the Beginning *3:42*
7. Forgiven *3:30*
8. Worthy After All *4:25*
9. I Am Holding You *3:48*
10. I Sing *3:37*

Produced and arranged by Mary Pay
Engineer and mixed by Ronnie Brookshire
The Drive Thru – Sound Stage (Nashville, TN)
The J Room – Sound Stage (Nashville, TN)
The Groove Room (Nashville, TN)

Additional Engineers:
Doug Delong, Patrick White, Jason Sheesley, Rodney Dawson, Tony Green, and Sid Greene
Mastered by Chad Evans,
Gaither Recording Studios (Alexandria, IN)

Drums, percussion/drum programming: Steve Brewster
Electric guitars: Jerry McPhearson
Electric & acoustic guitars: Mark Pay
Bass: Randy Melson
Piano & keyboards: Rolin Mains
Background vocals: Nichole Smith, Todd Smith, Shelly harris, Brent Henderson, Mark Pay
Strings:
The Nashville String Machine
Violin: Carl Gordetzkie, Pam Sixfin, Lee Larrison, Alan Umstead, Dave Davidson, David Angell
Cello: Bob Mason, John Catchings
String arrangements and conducting by Rolin Mains

For booking information, contact:
Todd Braschler
316-729-0223
tbraschler@hotmail.com
www.toddbraschlerministries.com